THE
GREATNESS
OF GOD'S POWER

RELEASING GOD'S POWER FOR DAILY LIVING

BY

Nancy Dufresne

EDM Publications

The Greatness of God's Power
ISBN: 978-0-940763-37-1
Copyright © 2013 by Ed Dufresne Ministries

Published by:
EDM Publishing
P.O. Box 1010
Murrieta, CA 92564
www.eddufresne.org

1st Printing: 5,000

Cover design: Nancy Dufresne & Grant Wilson
Cover Photo: © kaspargallery/shutterstock.com
Nancy Dufresne's Photo: Morgan Dufresne/© EDM Publishing

BOOKS BY DR. ED DUFRESNE

Praying God's Word

Devil, Don't Touch My Stuff!

There's a Healer in the House

Faithfulness: The Road to Divine Promotion

The Footsteps of a Prophet

Golden Nuggets for Longevity

Things that Pertain to the Spirit

How to be Rich God's Way

How to Flow with Anointings & Mantles

BOOKS BY NANCY DUFRESNE

Daily Healing Bread from God's Table

His Presence Shall be My Dwelling Place

Victory in the Name

There Came a Sound From Heaven: The Life Story of Dr. Ed Dufresne

The Healer Divine

Visitations from God

Responding to the Holy Spirit

God: The Revealer of Secrets

A Supernatural Prayer Life

Causes

I Have a Supply

Fit for the Master's Use: A Handbook for Raising Godly Children

A Sound, Disciplined Mind

Knowing Your Measure of Faith

CONTENTS

Chapter One

THE POWER THAT IS OURS

Wherefore I also, after I heard of your faith in the Lord Jesus, and love unto all the saints,

Cease not to give thanks for you, making mention of you in my prayers;

That the God of our Lord Jesus Christ, the Father of glory, may give unto you the spirit of wisdom and revelation in the knowledge of him:

The eyes of your understanding being enlightened; that ye may know what is the hope of his calling, and what the riches of the glory of his inheritance in the saints,

And what is the EXCEEDING greatness of His power to us-ward who believe...

— Ephesians 1:15-19

Paul records this prayer that the Spirit of God inspired him to pray for other believers. One of the things he prayed for them was that God would give them the spirit of wisdom and revelation in the knowledge of Him – that they would have revelation knowledge of:

> 1) who they are in Christ – *"...that you may know...what is the hope of his calling..."* (vs. 18)

> 2) all that belongs to them because they are in Christ – *"...that you may know...what the riches of the glory of his inheritance in the saints"* (vs. 18)

> 3) what they can do because they are in Christ – *"...that you may know...what is the exceeding greatness of his power to us-ward who believe..."* (vs. 19)

The wisdom of God is who you are in Christ. The wisdom God gives is to reveal to you who you are in Christ. As you learn and exercise your rights and privileges in Christ, you are moving in the wisdom of God.

When faced with a need, the way God helps you is to show you who you are in Christ and how all your needs are supplied in Him, and then your faith can lay hold of that supply and bring it to your need. With words of faith you can call that supply into your life.

Paul also prayed, *"The eyes of your understanding being enlightened...."* Your spirit has eyes, and Paul knew that this wisdom and revelation has to be seen with the eyes of your spirit before it will make a difference in your life. The intellect of man can't grasp these great truths that the Spirit longs to give; they must be received by the spirit of man. Once these mighty truths of who you are in Christ dawn on your spirit, life will be different for you.

The Amplified Bible reads, *"...having the eyes of your heart FLOODED with light, so that you can know and understand... "* (Ephesians 1:18). In a flood, things are removed from their place. When the eyes of your heart are flooded with wisdom and revelation, it will remove wrong thinking and wrong believing. When you think right and believe right, then you receive right things. All fear and doubt is dismissed when you think right and when you know who you are in Christ and walk in your authority.

To gain revelation that divine healing and divine health belongs to you because you are in Christ is to come into the wisdom of God. To gain revelation that prosperity and supply belong to you because you are in Christ is to move into the wisdom of God. Each time that you gain revelation of something more that belongs to you because you are in Christ, you move further into the wisdom of God. But these truths must reach into your spirit before they will flow as God intended.

If we are to grow and mature spiritually, we must have the spirit of wisdom and revelation of who we are in Christ and of His Word. It is not going to be imparted through our intellect. The Holy Spirit must unveil these truths to our spirits. When the spirit of wisdom and revelation is flowing, things will open up to us and we will see things we've never seen before.

GREAT KNOWLEDGE COMES
THROUGH THE WORD

God works in the earth through knowledge; He can't work through ignorance. To receive from God, you have to gain knowledge of how He works, and then walk in the light of that knowledge. The devil works in the earth through ignorance. When people are ignorant of the Word of God and how God works, then the enemy can work unhindered.

The devil is counting on the ignorance of man to work his plan against them. Hosea 4:6 tells us, *"My people are destroyed for lack of knowledge...."* The word "destroyed" means cut off. God's people are cut off from the blessings of God through the lack of knowledge. Notice that this verse doesn't say that God's people are destroyed because of the devil or because of opposition, but because of the lack of knowledge of God's Word. God's Word reveals how God works. When people are ignorant of how God works, then the enemy can gain the advantage over them. But as we gain knowledge of the Word of God, we can keep the door closed to the enemy.

Great faith comes with great knowledge of God, and great knowledge of God comes through His Word. We don't pray for faith, for faith comes by hearing the Word, but we do pray for greater knowledge of God's Word – that God would give us the spirit of wisdom and revelation in the knowledge of Him (Ephesians 1:17). Paul prayed this prayer for other believers, but you can also pray this or claim these things over your own life.

God longs for us to have the spirit of wisdom and revelation in the knowledge of Him, so I claim these things for my own life. Regularly I say, "I *take* unto myself the spirit of wisdom and revelation in the knowledge of Him. The eyes of my understanding are being enlightened; that I may know what is the hope of His calling, what is the riches of the glory of His inheritance in me, and I know what is the exceeding greatness of His power toward me, for I believe."

As I said, you can pray this prayer over your own life, or you can claim it for yourself. But you can't claim things for others like you can for yourself, so when it comes to others, you need to pray this for them. In fact, this is one of the best ways to pray for other believers.

The prayers in Ephesians 1:16-19 and Ephesians 3:14-21, as well as other prayers recorded in the epistles, are to be prayed regularly for other believers. (The epistles are the New Testament books starting with the book of Acts through the book of Revelation.) As you pray, claiming these Ephesian prayers for yourself, you will move into wisdom and revelation you've never had before. As you pray these prayers for others, even inserting their names into these verses, then God will move to show them things they have never seen before.

GOD'S POWER IS IN OUR DIRECTION

In Ephesians 1:18 & 19, Paul listed three things that he

prayed the saints would see:

1. That they may know what is the hope of
   His calling.
2. That they would know the riches of the
   glory of His inheritance in the saints.
3. They would know what is the exceeding
   greatness of His power to us-ward who
   believe.

I want to especially focus on this third point –
*"...that ye may know...what is the exceeding greatness of His
power to us-ward who believe."*

God's great power is *"...to us-ward who believe."* God's
power is in our direction – it's to us-ward. God's power toward us is ever present and at our disposal to draw upon
as it's needed; it's our faith that gives it action, releasing its
movement into our lives.

The *"...exceeding greatness of His power...."* To describe
God's power, Paul heaped adjective upon adjective – exceeding, greatness. It's an "exceeding" power. It exceeds all other
power – all demon power, all human power, all mental power, all physical power – it exceeds them all.

The word "exceed" means to go beyond the limit or measure of, to be greater than or superior to, to surpass, more
than sufficient.

All other powers have their limits – God's power is without limits. It's superior to all other powers – God's power knows no equal. It's a power that's more than sufficient to accomplish its task. It's a power that surpasses all other power. No power is a close second. God's power is so far out in front of and beyond all other powers, that it knows no equal. None other power is worthy of comparison. It's an exceeding power – exceeding all others. This exceeding power exceeds any need you'll ever face. Even though your need may appear to be great, God's power exceeds the need. His power is more than enough to supply every need, for His power that's in our direction exceeds all.

"...The exceeding GREATNESS of His power...." God's power is a greater power. Since it's a greater power, remember that all other powers are a lesser power. The enemy's power is lesser – always lesser. Human power, mental power, physical powers are all lesser powers. But we're not confined to live according to our own lesser human, mental, physical power – we have an exceeding, greater power to draw on, for it's in our direction. This exceeding, greater power is at our disposal – it's to us-ward.

RESURRECTION POWER

EPHESIANS 1:19-23
19 (That you may know) **what is the exceeding greatness of his power to us-ward who believe, according to the working of his mighty power,**
20 Which he wrought in Christ, when he raised

him from the dead, and set him at his own right
hand in the heavenly places.
21 Far above all principality, and power, and
might, and dominion, and every name that is
named, not only in this world, but also in that
which is to come.
22 And hath put all things under his feet, and
gave him to be the head over all things to the
church.
23 Which is his body, the fullness of him that
filleth all in all.

Look again at verses 19 & 20. "(That you may know) *the
exceeding greatness of his power to us-ward who believe, according to the working of his mighty power, which he wrought
in Christ, WHEN HE RAISED HIM FROM THE DEAD....*"

When the Spirit of God moved upon Paul to describe the
exceeding greatness of God's power that's in our direction,
he didn't compare it to *creative* power that was in operation
when God created the heavens and the earth. He didn't compare it to *miracle* power that was in operation at the parting
of the Red Sea. He didn't compare it to *healing* power that
flowed when Jesus healed the multitudes. He didn't compare
it to *multiplication* power that moved when Jesus multiplied
the loaves and the fish. What did the Spirit of God compare
the great power that is in our direction to? Resurrection power! The same power that raised Jesus from the dead is the
same power that is in our direction and at our disposal. This
power is to us-ward who believe – it's waiting on our faith! As
we release faith in this power, it will work in our behalf.

As Ephesians 1:21 tells us, Jesus was raised, *"FAR ABOVE all principality, and power, and might, and dominion...."* All these evil powers opposed His resurrection. But so great was this mighty resurrection power that raised Jesus, that all their combined might and efforts proved as nothing in comparison to the exceeding greatness of God's power.

Not only did this mighty resurrection power defeat death and raise Jesus beyond all the opposing powers of hell, but that same power carried Him all the way to Heaven and seated Him victoriously on the throne, at the right hand of God to be the imperial Head of the Church. Power did that for Jesus – power did that for us – for our benefit!

Now, since God's great resurrection power accomplished this great, all-conquering work, what will it do for you? Is it not enough for your own needs? Is it not enough to turn your situation? Is it not enough to supply your needs? Is it not enough to change impossibilities to possibilities? Absolutely, it is! It is more than enough!

Because of this exceeding, great, all-conquering power, we are not suited to be beneath – only above! We have been raised with Jesus, and we too are now seated *far above* all opposition. We are in the victory seat! Our authority stems from that victory seat! (Eph. 2:5,6)

Chapter Two

VICTORY IS OURS

For if by one man's offence (Adam's sin) *death reigned by one; much more they which receive abundance of grace and of the gift of righteousness shall REIGN IN LIFE by one, Jesus Christ.*

— Romans 5:17

Everything that Jesus did, He did for our benefit — for the benefit of the Church, God's people. Jesus defeated the enemy in our behalf, for our benefit. His victory is our victory. The victory He won has been credited to us; it is as though we defeated the enemy. Christ did it in our stead.

Satan has no more authority over our lives; therefore, we are to *reign in life.* We are to rule and reign over the circumstances in our lives instead of circumstances ruling and reigning over us. God has assigned us and authorized us to reign in life. If you are to reign over the circumstances in life, you must know your authority over the enemy and exercise that authority or he will take advantage of you.

Jesus conquered Satan in His death, burial and resurrection for Colossians 2:15 reads, *"And having spoiled prin-*

cipalities and powers, he made a shew of them openly, TRI-UMPHING OVER THEM in it (the Cross)."

Colossians 2:15 (Conybeare), *"...He DISARMED the principalities and powers...."*

Colossians 2:15 (Phillips), *"...he EXPOSED THEM, SHATTERED, EMPTY, AND DEFEATED, in his final glorious triumphant act!"*

Satan and all the evil spirits opposed Jesus, but Jesus disarmed and exposed them as being shattered, empty and defeated. Satan's defeat is total and complete. Jesus reduced them to nothing. We do not have to defeat Satan, for he is a defeated foe.

The wisdom of God that we are to receive is that Jesus' defeat of the enemy is complete, and we only have to stand our ground on God's Word, enforcing the victory Jesus won for us, and enforcing Satan's defeated position.

We don't have to *get* victory – victory is ours! I don't have to *get* anything that Jesus has provided for me – all is mine! Victory is mine, healing is mine, prosperity is mine, joy, peace and all of Heaven's blessings *are* mine. I don't have to *get* them – they are my present possession – they are mine *now.*

As our minds are renewed with these truths, and as we act on them in the face of all opposition, tests, and trials, then this victory becomes a reality in our lives.

We are to approach all opposition and tests with the con-

sciousness that through Christ we have total and complete
authority over Satan and every evil spirit, for the Lord Jesus
Christ defeated him for us.

THE GOOD FIGHT OF FAITH

We are to fight the good fight of faith, which is the only
fight the believer is to be engaged in. The good fight of faith
is taking our stand on God's Word in the face of all opposing circumstances, and refusing to believe or speak anything
that contradicts God's Word. Satan uses circumstances, situations, and feelings to try to get us to change what we believe, but we refuse to let them change what we believe about
God's Word. We take our stand on God's Word and hold fast
to confessing it in the face of all that we may see, hear and
feel. The good fight of faith is a fight of words – holding fast
to believing and speaking God's Word in the face of all opposition.

We don't fight the devil – he's defeated. We fight to stand
on and hold to God's Word, refusing to be swayed off it. This
is the good fight of faith, for it's the winning fight. Every
other fight is a losing fight. Worry is a losing fight. Doubt is
a losing fight. The mental fight is a losing fight.

Faith is of the heart, and as we continue to speak faith
words, regardless of what may be coming against us and our
minds, we enforce the victory that is ours as we fight the
good fight of faith.

Satan seeks to blind us, and all believers, to the truth that he's been dethroned so that he can work unhindered against our lives. But when we see these things for ourselves, and when we pray for other believers, as Paul did (in Ephesians 1:16-19) that the eyes of their understanding would be enlightened to see these things, that's when believers will begin to experience this victory that Jesus provided for us. When we see the truth of Satan's absolute and total defeat, and our authority over him, that's when we will reign in life as a king.

Chapter Three

THE HOLY SPIRIT'S ENTRANCE

On one occasion, Jesus appeared to my spiritual father, and in that vision, Jesus stated, "When I was on the earth, I was the power of God. If people needed God's power, they had to get to where I was. That's why the multitudes thronged Me to touch Me. They had to touch Me to touch power. But now the Holy Spirit is present on the earth and *He* is the power of God. He is present everywhere, so power is present everywhere." Jesus went on to say, "There's enough power in every sick room, in every hospital room to raise up that sick one, if they only knew it was present and would give it action."

The Holy Spirit has not always been a resident on the earth, but on the day of Pentecost, He left Heaven to dwell on the earth so He could indwell the Church and every child of God. Jesus told His disciples, *"Nevertheless I tell you the truth; it is expedient* (profitable) *for you that I go away: for if I go not away, the Comforter will not come unto you; but if I depart, I WILL SEND HIM UNTO YOU"* (John 16:7). In this scripture, Jesus called the Holy Spirit the Comforter. John 14:16 tells us, *"And I* (Jesus) *will pray the Father, and he shall give you another Comforter, that he may abide with you for ever.*" Jesus is the gift to the whole world, but there is a gift that belongs only to the child of God – the Person of the Holy Spirit. You must be born again to receive this wonderful gift.

Jesus told the disciples that it was better for Him to leave the earth and return to Heaven rather than to stay with them. Why would it be better for Him to leave than stay? For by returning to Heaven, He would ask the Father to send the Holy Spirit to the earth and the Father would send Him.

Although Jesus is the Son of God, while He was on the earth, He was confined to a human body; therefore, the power of God was limited to a human body. But because the Holy Spirit is a Spirit, He isn't limited to a human body like Jesus was. He is present everywhere; therefore, the power of God is now present everywhere. That's why Jesus said it was expedient, more profitable for the disciples that He return to Heaven, for then the Holy Spirit would be sent to dwell in and with them.

John 14:16 tells us, *"And I* (Jesus) *will pray the Father, and he shall give you ANOTHER Comforter, that he may abide with you forever."* In this word "another" we see the best description of the Holy Spirit. If I asked a friend to loan me money, and they handed me a $5 bill, but I said, "That won't be enough money. Would you give me another?" If they handed me a $1 bill, they didn't give me another. If they handed me a $10 bill, they didn't give me another. If they were to give me another, they would have to give me the same thing they initially gave me.

Likewise, when Jesus told the disciples that God would give them "another" Comforter, then He would have to be just like Jesus, or He wouldn't be "another". Everything Jesus was to the disciples when He was on the earth, the Holy Spirit would be to them when He arrived on the earth. They would not be left with less when Jesus returned to Heaven and the Holy Spirit arrived, for He is "another", just like Jesus.

Jesus said it was expedient (profitable), for them that He leave and the Holy Spirit come, for the Holy Spirit would be to them everything Jesus was to them, but better, in the sense that Jesus couldn't be with them 24 hours a day since He was limited to a human body. But the Holy Spirit would dwell in them and with them, and would abide with them forever; He would always be with them.

The Amplified translation of John 14:16 says the word "Comforter" means Counselor, Helper, Intercessor, Advocate, Strengthener, and Standby. The Holy Spirit is all these things to us, and He will always be with us; we are never without Him and all that He is.

On the day of Pentecost, the Holy Spirit made His entrance to the earth. Up until that time, the earth had never been the dwelling place of the Holy Spirit. The anointing of God would come on certain individuals of the Old Testament to empower them to fulfill a specific work, but He never dwelt in them. Even when Jesus was baptized in the Jordan River, the Holy Spirit had to come down from Heaven upon Him in the form of a dove because the Holy Spirit was not yet a resident on the earth. But on the day of Pentecost, the Holy Spirit made His entrance to reside upon the earth to be the ever-present companion of the Church, the Body of Christ.

After Jesus' death, burial and resurrection, He appeared to His disciples and gave them instructions.

> **ACTS 1:4, 5 & 8**
> **4 And being assembled together with them, (Jesus) commanded them that they should not depart from Jerusalem, but wait for the promise of the Father, which, saith he, ye have heard of me.**
> **5 For John truly baptized with water; but ye shall be baptized with the Holy Ghost not many days hence.**
> **8 But ye shall receive POWER, after that the Holy Ghost is come upon you: and ye shall be witnesses unto me both in Jerusalem, and in all Judaea, and in Samaria, and unto the uttermost part of the earth.**

As Jesus instructed, 120 disciples assembled together to wait for the Holy Spirit's great entrance upon the earth.

> **ACTS 2:1-4**
> **1 And when the day of Pentecost was fully come, they were all with one accord in one place.**

2 And suddenly there came a sound from heaven as of a rushing mighty wind, and it filled all the house where they were sitting.
3 And there appeared unto them cloven tongues like as of fire, and it sat upon each of them.
4 And they were all filled with the Holy Ghost, and began to speak with other tongues, as the Spirit gave them utterance.

They were waiting for Him – they were expecting His entrance. The Holy Spirit couldn't make His entrance just anywhere – He had to enter where faith was waiting for Him. Every movement of God must be met with faith, including the entrance of the Holy Spirit. There were 120 believers assembled together, expecting His entrance. Their faith invited His presence to fill the earth, as well as to indwell them.

The Holy Spirit's entrance thundered into earth's atmosphere with a great sound. *"And suddenly there came a sound from heaven as of a rushing mighty wind, and it filled all the house where they were sitting"* (Acts 2:2). The totality of the Spirit landed in that upper room with a mighty sound; then the Spirit's mighty presence moved from that upper room throughout the whole earth. So great was the sound of the Spirit's entrance that the sound was heard throughout the city and the multitude came together to see what made the sound (Acts 2:6). The disciples came out of that upper room, now filled with the Holy Spirit, and met the great multitude that had gathered because of the sound. It was from there that Peter preached the great sermon to the multitude that brought thousands to salvation, and the Church was born (Acts 2:14-47).

The Holy Spirit's presence moved from the upper room and went throughout the whole earth. Because the Holy Spirit is present everywhere, the power of God is present everywhere, for He is the power of God. That's why a person can be saved anywhere; they don't have to be in a church to receive Jesus, for the power to be saved is everywhere. A person can be healed anywhere, for healing power is everywhere. Power for all these things is present everywhere, for the Holy Spirit is present everywhere.

That's why Jesus stated in that vision to my spiritual father, "There's enough power in every sick room and in every hospital room to raise up that sick one, if they only knew it was present and would give it action." Power is present everywhere, for the Holy Spirit is present everywhere.

Although the power of God is present everywhere, it's not moving or in manifestation everywhere, for it requires faith to bring that power into manifestation. For God's power to flow, someone must know that it's present, and must give it action by releasing faith in the power of God, for faith gives it action.

The Spirit Within & the Spirit Upon

In John 14:17 Jesus told the disciples that the Holy Spirit would dwell with them and would be IN them. But in

Acts 1:8 Jesus told the disciples, *"But ye shall receive POWER, after that the Holy Ghost is come UPON you: and ye shall be WITNESSES unto me both in Jerusalem, and in all Judaea, and in Samaria, and unto the uttermost part of the earth"* (Acts 1:8).

The Holy Ghost is the gift that dwells *in* the believer, but He is also the power of God that comes *upon* a minister to help him fulfill his ministry, for Jesus told His disciples that the power of the Holy Ghost would come upon them to be His witnesses. The Holy Spirit's power will not only come upon a fivefold minister, but will come upon any believer to enable him to fulfill a special work God calls him to, or to fulfill whatever call is on his life.

The Holy Spirit is our ever-present Comforter, Helper, Teacher, Guide, Counselor, Advocate, and Standby. He is the power of God present within us, and His power is ever at our disposal to enable us to fulfill what God has called us to and to help us to live victorious in this life. His power *within* us enables us to live a life of victory. His power that comes *upon* us enables us to be a witness to others, equipping us for service, to minister to and bless others.

THE INDWELLING & THE INFILLING

At the new birth, the Holy Spirit imparted God's life and nature into your spirit, and your spirit was born again. God didn't heal your old spirit, but He gave you a brand new spirit. God's Word tells us, *"Therefore if any man be in Christ, he is a NEW CREATURE: old things are passed away; behold, all things are become new"* (II Corinthians 5:17).

At the new birth, the Holy Spirit came to *indwell* you. But Acts 2 tells of an additional experience that belongs to every child of God, and that is the *infilling* of the Holy Spirit.

The 120 disciples were gathered in the upper room waiting for the Holy Spirit's arrival; they were assembled there, as Jesus told them, so they could receive the *infilling* of the Holy Spirit. When the Holy Spirit entered that room, they were all *filled* with the Holy Ghost and began to speak with other tongues (Acts 2:4). To receive the *infilling* of the Holy Spirit is to receive a deeper dimension of God. In receiving the infilling of the Holy Spirit, they were now empowered by the Holy Spirit to fulfill their calls; they were empowered for service.

When you're born again, you receive the *indwelling* of the Spirit; the Holy Spirit dwells in you. The *indwelling* of the Spirit is like having one drink of water, but just having one drink of water is no sign you're full of water. There is also the *infilling* of the Spirit that God wants for all His children, where you drink in the fullness of the Spirit; you go from the *indwelling* to the *infilling* of the Spirit.

Once you're filled with the Spirit, it's evidenced by speaking in tongues. When you get full of the Spirit, it flows out and the Spirit gives utterance in other tongues, and you speak out those utterances He gives. (To receive the infilling of the Holy Spirit, see the instruction given on page 89.)

To be born again is to receive the life and nature of God, but to be filled with the Holy Spirit with the evidence of speaking in other tongues is to move into God's supernatural power. Once you're filled with the Spirit, you will experience God's supernatural power in a greater measure.

Chapter Four

THE POWER OF GOD
IN MANIFESTATION

*Cease not to give thanks for you, making men-
tion of you in my prayers;*

*That the God of our Lord Jesus Christ, the Fa-
ther of glory, may give unto you the spirit of wisdom
and revelation in the knowledge of him:*

*The eyes of your understanding being enlight-
ened; that ye may know what is the hope of his calling, and what the riches of the glory of his inheritance in the saints,*

*And what is the exceeding greatness of his power
to us-ward who believe...*

– Ephesians 1:16-19

In the vision that my spiritual father had of Jesus, He
stated that there is enough power in every sick room and in
every hospital room to raise up that sick one, if they only knew
that it was present and would give it action. So according to
what Jesus said, we must know two things:

1. That God's power is present

2. How to give that power action or how to
   bring it into manifestation

In the previous chapters, we've shown through God's Word that His power is present, so we know it's present. Now, let's look at how to give it action, or how to bring it into manifestation.

Ephesians 1:19 tells us that the exceeding greatness of God's power is toward us who believe – we must believe in the power of God.

What is it that gives action to God's power, bringing it into manifestation? Faith! We must release our faith in the power of God. Paul wrote saying, *"That your FAITH should not stand in the wisdom of men, but in the POWER of God."* (I Corinthians 2:5). Don't put your faith in what the mind of man can figure out or calculate, rather, put your faith in God's power.

Hebrews 4:2 tells us about the Hebrews that wandered in the wilderness for forty years after God delivered them out of Egypt. *"For unto us was the gospel preached, as well as unto them: but the word preached did not profit them, not being MIXED WITH FAITH in them that heard it."* Is it really possible for the Word to be preached and a person not profit from it? Yes. If the hearer doesn't mix their faith with the Word they've heard preached, they won't profit or gain anything from it. Faith must be mixed with the Word.

How do you mix faith with the Word? Your tongue is the mixer. When the Word is preached, faith comes in your heart. But the faith in your heart must be released for it to benefit you. The faith in your heart is released through what you say and do.

God's Word tells us that faith comes by hearing what God's Word says (Romans 10:17). Although faith *comes* by hearing, faith doesn't *operate* by hearing – faith isn't *released* by hearing – it's released by speaking. For Romans 10:10 tells us, *"For with the HEART man believeth unto righteousness; and with the MOUTH confession is made unto salvation* (or unto the manifestation of what you're believing for).*"* Faith must be in two places if it is to work – in your heart and in your mouth. You can have faith in your heart, but if you never speak words of faith, your faith will never work for you. When you *hear* the Word, you *believe*. And when you *speak* the Word, you *receive*.

How long do you have to speak the Word? Until what you're believing for comes into manifestation.

For the Word to benefit you, you must mix faith with it. Your tongue is the mixer – mixing the faith that's in your heart with the Word that's in your mouth.

For example, God's Word tells us that Jesus took our infirmities and bare our sicknesses, and that by His stripes we were healed (Matthew 8:17 & I Peter 2:24). We believe that, so we are to say with our own mouth, "Jesus took my infirmities and bare my sickness, and by His stripes I was healed. Therefore, I am healed now." Continue to make that confession until healing comes into manifestation, regardless of how long it takes. That's how you mix faith with the Word.

God's Word also tells us, *"But my God shall supply all your need according to his riches in glory by Christ Jesus"* (Philippians 4:19). We believe that, so we are to put it in our mouth, no matter what our circumstances may be; we declare that God supplies all our needs according to His riches in glory by Christ Jesus. Continue to make that confession until the supply comes into manifestation. That's how you mix faith with the Word.

MIXING FAITH WITH POWER

Just as faith must be mixed with the Word for it to work in your life, faith must be mixed with the power of God for that power to work.

Paul told us that the exceeding greatness of God's power is to us-ward who believe. It is in our direction. We are possessors of God's power now, but it's faith that causes it to come into manifestation. Just because God's power is present doesn't mean it's in manifestation. For it to come into manifestation, someone must mix faith with the power that's present.

God's power is at our disposal to use as we need it. We are stewards of God's power, and we can draw upon it whenever we need it. Many are waiting for God to send His power to their situation, for they are waiting on *God* to *initiate* something in their behalf. But for those of us who have our spiritual understanding enlightened, we see that power is already present and at our disposal to draw upon. *WE are authorized to INITIATE the flow of God's power when we need it.* We're not waiting on God, for power is waiting on us to release our faith.

I have come to see that 95% of what we receive from God is initiated by us, not by God. Because He has empowered us and authorized us, we can release faith in God's power and receive the flow of that power when it's needed.

POWER IN EVERY SICK ROOM

As I stated previously, in the vision that my spiritual father had of Jesus, He stated that there is enough power in every sick room and in every hospital room to raise up that sick one, if they only knew that it was present and would give it action. So according to what Jesus said, we must know two things:

1. That God's power is present

2. How to give that power action or how to
   bring it into manifestation

Years ago, when our youngest son was a newborn, he was having problems in his lungs, so I took him to the doctor. The doctor admitted him immediately to the hospital, wanting to run further tests. When they got him settled into the hospital room, the nurse came in and told me that the doctor was going to be delayed for about an hour. He instructed the nurses not to give our son any medication, although he had a high fever, because he didn't want to alter the symptoms until he had a chance to examine him further.

After the nurse left, I held our son, rocking him in the rocking chair. As I rocked, I said, "Jesus, You appeared to my spiritual father and told him that there is enough power in every sick room and in every hospital room to raise up that sick one, if they only knew that power was present and would give it action. Jesus, I'm in one of those hospital rooms. I believe what You said; I believe that the power to heal our son is present, so I give it action. I release my faith in Your Word. I speak for that power that is present to move into our son's body and work a cure. I believe by faith that power is working now, and I thank You for it." Then I just spent the next 45 minutes praising God, thanking Him that His power was working in our son's body.

After that, the doctor arrived and began his examination. He said, "All the fever is gone and I can't find any more symptoms." Our son was healed!

I knew the power of God was present because the Holy Spirit was present. I then gave that power action through the words I spoke, and then I praised God for His power that was at work in our son's body.

Stir Up the Gift

Power is present, but it's waiting on someone to release

faith in it, then we will see it flow.

Many pray for God to send power for revival, for miracles, and healings, but God's not withholding power — we don't have to coerce power from His hand; He wants people to receive of His power. He already sent His power when He sent the Holy Ghost to the earth; therefore, power is present everywhere. The greatness of His power is in us, and it's in our direction. Power is present, but it's waiting on someone to release faith in it, then we will see it flow.

We don't need to pray for God to send the power, but we need to do what Paul told Timothy, *"...I would remind you to STIR UP (rekindle the embers of, fan the flame of, and keep burning) the [gracious] gift of God, [the inner fire] that is in you... "* (II Timothy 1:6, Amplified). Believers just need to stir up the gift, the fire on the inside of them, the Holy Ghost, and be bold to release faith in God's power that is already present.

Notice a prayer the disciples prayed, *"...grant unto thy servants, that with all BOLDNESS they may speak thy word, by stretching forth thine HAND to heal; and that signs and wonders may be done by the name of thy holy child Jesus"* (Acts 4:29 & 30). They didn't pray that God would give them power, for they understood that they had power. But they prayed for boldness. Be bold to act on the power that's already present.

The disciples prayer also stated, *"...stretching forth thine HAND to heal...."* The hand is a part of the body. Jesus is the

Head, but believers are the *Body* of Christ. Our hands are the hands that God is going to stretch forth. He needs us to yield to and cooperate with Him so His power can heal and work miracles. We must be bold to act on the power of God that's present to heal – that's how God stretches forth His hand to heal. Signs and wonders will come to pass the same way – as we boldly act on and cooperate with God's power that's already present.

A Divine Explosion

In a scientist's or chemist's laboratory, there are different liquids and chemicals that are stored in individual beakers. As long as they're stored separately, there's no reaction. But if they mix certain chemicals together, they can get quite an explosion.

Likewise, God's power will remain inactive as long as it stands alone. But if you will mix faith with it, you will get a *divine* explosion that will bring benefit. Many are praying for God's power to explode into their situation, but His power is waiting for them to mix faith with it. When this is done, power will do its mighty work.

The Power is Present

Years ago, I had spent several weeks teaching our congregation that the power of God is always present to meet their needs and that they don't have to wait until the next church service to be prayed for. They can receive of God's power right where they're at – whether they are in their car, in their home, or in their office on their job – the power of God is present everywhere; it's present right where they are.

But one particular Sunday morning, as I got up to continue preaching along this line, I heard myself say repeatedly as I walked back and forth across the platform, "Let the power fall! Let the power fall!" As I heard these words coming out of my mouth, I started having a conversation inwardly with God. I asked, "Have I been teaching this wrong? I've been teaching the people that the power of God is present, so why am I saying 'Let the power fall!' Isn't it already here?"

God answered me, "Yes, the power is present, but just because it's present doesn't mean that it's moving." In a flash I saw it as He gave me an illustration. He said, "At a child's birthday party, sometimes there is a piñata (a cardboard figure filled with candy and treats). That piñata is hung in a high place. It's present, but just because it's present doesn't mean that any of the kids are getting any of the goodies inside it. But as a child hits that piñata with a stick, the piñata breaks open and the treats inside flow out, then all the kids gather up the goodies."

"Likewise," God continued, "although power is present everywhere, no one will benefit from it or receive anything from it until someone strikes it. *Words of faith are the stick that strikes the power of God. When someone speaks words of faith, power is released to flow into their need or situation."*

When a child hits a piñata just right with the stick and all the treats fall out, the child that hit it isn't the only one who gets to gather up the goodies, but all the kids present get to gather them up – even though they aren't the ones that struck it.

Even so, with the power of God. It may be the faith of one person present who strikes the power of God, causing it to flow. But once it's flowing, all those present have the opportunity to gather it up. With their own faith they can reach out and receive of that power that's flowing. The power that's present won't benefit anyone until someone strikes that power with their words of faith, causing it to flow and to come into manifestation.

PREPARING THE ATMOSPHERE

One preacher told the story of their Pentecostal grandmother who got saved in the early 1900s. Before a church service, several grandmas would arrive at the church an hour early. They would gather to pray and worship God in their church sanctuary. They didn't have any carpet in their building, just an old wooden floor. They didn't have any chairs. If they wanted a chair, they had to bring one from home. They didn't have a sound system or any instruments. But as these grandmas would start worshipping God, the anointing would fall. One of them would tap their foot on the floor, but they did it under the anointing. As one grandma would tap a beat with her foot, another grandmother would add her part and start singing under the anointing. Then the power of God would begin moving mightily in that building. What were they doing? They were striking the power of God that was present and getting it flowing – then the atmosphere would be charged with the power of God.

When the rest of the congregation arrived, they would step into that atmosphere that was already charged with the power of God. Then those who had a need could simply reach out with their faith and lay hold on that power that was already flowing. Although the rest of the congregation weren't the ones who initially struck the power of God, causing it to flow, they could simply reach out with their faith and gather it up for their own need. How would they receive of that power? By speaking words like, "I receive that power." Then it would move into their life.

We need to realize that God's power is already present. We don't have to ask Him to send His power, but we do have to release faith in God's power that is present through the words we speak, causing it to flow and bringing it into manifestation.

"I Know That You Know That I Know!"

This same preacher told another story about this same grandma and her grown daughter who lived in the same town. One day, as this grandma was at home, there was a knock on her door. When she opened the door, a doctor was standing there and said, "I have your daughter in the back seat of my car. Her appendix has burst, and I am driving her to the hospital. But since the hospital is some distance away, she will die before I can get her there, so I am stopping by to let you see her one last time."

The grandma answered, "No, I don't want to see her. You just take her on to the hospital." She shut the door, and as the doctor drove off, she stood in her home and lifted her heart to God and said, "God, I want You to know, that I know that You know that I know!" What a prayer! She was letting God know that she knew what His Word says and she was holding to what she knew. A few minutes later there was another knock at the door. When she opened it, the doctor stood there with her daughter, who was raised up completely whole.

What did this grandma do? She struck the power of God with her faith, and when she did, that power flowed and worked healing in her daughter's body.

God's power is present and it's waiting on your faith. When you mix your faith with it, it will do its mighty work.

Chapter Five

I BELIEVE I RECEIVE

When it comes to our victory, we must understand that we have a part to play and God has a part to play. Our part is to release faith in God's power, and God's part is to manifest by His power, the answer and the supply we may need. We are not the one who manifests the answer, He is. As we do our part, the believing, He will do His part, the manifesting.

The Holy Ghost is the Manifestor, not us. So, we are not to touch the manifestation in our thought life, that's not our part. We must not think about or say, "When is the answer going to manifest? How is He going to do it? Why hasn't it manifested yet?" If we do, we are intruding into God's part because the manifestation of the answer is His part, not ours. We aren't capable of fulfilling His part – only He can do that. However, we are capable of doing our part, which is to believe that His power is working in our behalf, regardless of what we may see, feel or hear.

Mark 11:24 tells us, *"Therefore I say unto you, What things soever ye desire, when ye pray, believe that ye receive them* (our part), *and ye shall have them* (God's part)."

Mark 11:24 spells out our part:

1. Desire

2. Pray

3. Believe we receive at the time we pray

This verse also spells out God's part: *"...and ye shall have them."* This is referring to the manifestation of your answer. God is the One who manifests what we believe. So, don't even touch the manifestation in your thought life. Don't ask, "When is God going to do it?" or "How is God going to do it?" Just focus on doing *your* part, and when you do, He is faithful to fulfill His part.

RECEIVING & MANIFESTATION – TWO DIFFERENT THINGS

Where some may misunderstand Mark 11:24 is with the word "receive". *"...What things soever ye desire, when ye pray, believe that ye RECEIVE them, and ye shall have them."* It doesn't say to believe it's *manifested*, but we are to believe we *receive* it. Receiving and manifestation are two different things. Receiving is of the spirit realm, the faith realm. Manifestation is of the natural realm. Receiving is what you do with your spirit by faith. We are to believe that we *receive* at the time we pray. God isn't asking us to believe something is *manifested* that isn't, but He is instructing us to believe we *receive* it – that He has made it ours and that it is moving into our lives now, before we see it. We receive with our spirits, and when we do, then it will manifest in this natural arena.

Faith is for the unseen; faith will believe that it receives while the answer is yet unseen.

Your answer exists in two forms: the unseen form and the seen form. Faith believes with the heart that it receives the answer while it is still in its unseen form; the mind can't believe that, but the heart, or the spirit of man can. When you believe with your spirit and say with your mouth that you believe you receive your answer while it is still in its unseen form, then it will move from its unseen form into its seen form – it will manifest. We could correctly translate Mark 11:24 to read, "...*What things soever ye desire, when ye pray, believe* (with your spirit that) *ye receive* (your answer while it's still in its unseen form), *and ye shall have them* (they shall come into their seen form – they shall manifest)."

CAN'T BELIEVE GOD WITH THE MIND

Many stumble over this verse because they're trying to believe with their minds. But faith isn't in the mind of man – it's in the heart, or spirit, of man. The mind was not built to conduct faith or other spiritual things, but only natural things. When believers struggle with faith – struggle to receive, struggle to believe, start feeling desperate, and grasp to believe – it's because they're trying to believe God with their minds. The mind wasn't built to conduct faith.

Faith doesn't come from the mind of man, and the mind

can't conduct faith, but the mind can be renewed so that it agrees with the Word and the faith in the heart.

The natural mind that hasn't been renewed with the Word of God (which means to take God's thoughts and make them yours) will reason against and argue with the Word, and it will fight against the faith in the heart and shut that faith down. But the mind must be renewed with the Word of God so it will think in line with God's Word and agree with the faith in the heart instead of fighting against it.

You can't believe God with your mind; you can only believe God with your heart, your spirit. When believing God, you must quiet the mind and believe God with your spirit. The faith of God is in your spirit, not your mind. *Your spirit can believe what your mind can't understand or figure out.* To walk by faith, you must dip down into your spirit and ignore the mind, for the mind is not the conductor of faith.

When builders construct a home, they will have an electrician to wire the home with electrical wiring so that the house will have power. That electrician knows he can't use just any kind of material when wiring the house for electricity. He can't pull out a box of rubber bands and try to wire the house with them; although they're are a good, useful product, they won't conduct electricity. He has to use the proper materials if power is to flow.

Likewise, the mind is good and useful for natural things, but it was never intended to conduct faith. Your spirit is for conducting faith, and if you're to receive from God, you must receive with your spirit, or your heart.

If an electrician tries to wire a home with rubber bands, he and the homeowners are going to be sadly disappointed when they find that they won't conduct power.

Likewise, when believers try to believe with their minds, they will be sadly disappointed, because the mind can't conduct faith or God's power.

The electrician would be amiss in calling the power company to complain that they've done something wrong when he's the one who mis-wired the house. Likewise, someone is amiss to accuse God, His Word, the preacher, or faith of not working when they're trying to believe God with their mind. The fault doesn't lay with God or His Word, but with the one who's trying to believe God and conduct God's power with their mind, when the mind doesn't conduct faith.

When a house is properly wired and power is flowing to that house, it works every time. Likewise, when believers are believing God with their spirits, and not trying to believe God with their minds, and releasing that faith through the words they speak, it will work every time.

FLIP THE SWITCH OF FAITH

Now, if the electrician properly wired a home but the homeowner never flipped the light switch, power wouldn't flow; but then the power isn't the fault and can't be blamed. No, the switch must be flipped if power is to flow.

Likewise, God, has wired you with His power. Because the greater One is in you, you are wired with power, but you must still flip the switch of faith if the power that you're wired with is to flow. It's not God's part to flip the switch of faith – that's your part. God did His part by *wiring* you with power. He's put power at your disposal anytime you need it. All it's waiting on is for you to flip the switch.

Mark 11:24 tells us how to flip the switch, *"...What things soever ye desire, when ye pray, believe you receive them* (with your spirit), *and ye shall have them* (they shall manifest)." At the time we pray, we are to believe that God's power begins moving in our direction. When we believe that and hold fast to our confession of that while our answer is still in its unseen form, then it will manifest, *"... ye shall have them."* From the time we pray, we are to continually say, "I believe I receive my answer." When you do that, which is your part, then God, who is the Manifestor, will do His part. That's how you release your faith and give action to God's power.

Chapter Six

COOPERATING WITH GOD'S POWER

God's power brings great blessing to people's lives and situations, but we must learn how to cooperate with God and His power so people's lives can be blessed by it.

Power makes life better. Even in the natural realm, since man has learned the laws that govern electricity, the power of electricity has made life better, and more can be accomplished because of that power.

History tells us of certain men who searched out the laws that govern electricity so they could make it available to the masses. Benjamin Franklin was one of those men. History tells us of how Benjamin Franklin sent a kite with a key on the string up into the sky during a lightning storm. He recognized that lightning in the sky as power. He wondered if he could initiate contact with that power. In sending up the kite with the key on the string, it attracted the lightning to it, and he got a real charge! He was beginning to learn the laws that govern electricity. He had learned that he could attract the power of electricity to a particular location.

Other men began to search out these laws; among them was Thomas Edison. He knew we could initiate contact with power, but could we generate it, harness it, store it, and even direct it? As he conducted his experiments, he found out we could. Because of these men's research and knowledge of electrical power, great blessing has come to the masses, and changed the complexion of how life is lived on the earth.

Although electrical power has always been present on the earth, not until someone searched out the laws that govern it and cooperated with those laws did men benefit from it. Benjamin Franklin, Thomas Edison, and others weren't content to leave that power unaccessed, but they learned how to cooperate with it so the masses could be blessed. Likewise, God's power is present on the earth, and we must not be content to leave God's power unaccessed.

Men of God who have gone before us, have learned the laws that govern God's power, but *we* must also learn to become proficient with the laws that govern God's power. As we cooperate with God's power, then that power brings blessing to men. Just like electrical power makes life better, God's power makes life better.

The everyday duties, responsibilities, and activities of life are made easier and better with electrical power. Lighting, appliances, and other electrical equipment have made life so much better and different. Electrical appliances and equipment we use in getting dressed in the morning, in running our households, and in our offices and businesses allow us to accomplish things that would have been impossible without electrical power. Because of electrical power, we enjoy conveniences that would have been impossible otherwise.

Likewise, God's power makes life easier and brings the impossible into the realm of possibility. When we don't skillfully access and cooperate with the power of God in our everyday lives, then we forfeit power that would make life better and make the impossible possible.

We must learn the laws that govern the power of God and become skillful at accessing it in our everyday lives, and not just confine the flow of God's power to church services.

THE LAW OF FAITH

Romans 3:27 speaks of the law of faith.

Laws govern something. The law of gravity governs gravity. The law of lift governs the lift of aircraft. *The law of faith governs the flow of God's power.*

Some laws work automatically – like gravity. Gravity works for everyone and everything on earth, whether it's understood or not. But other laws have to be worked on purpose. For example, the law of lift that causes an airplane to lift off the ground has to be worked on purpose. As men discovered and learned to work with the law of lift, men left the earth and took to the skies. But man has to work that law on purpose.

Likewise, the law of faith, which governs the flow of the power of God, doesn't work automatically; it must be worked on purpose. Man must learn the law of faith and work that law so that the power of God can flow and bless the lives of people.

The power of God, like electricity, can be conducted, stored, and directed so that it flows to a particular person and need. But man must learn the law of faith so they can take steps of faith that cooperate with that power, allowing it to flow and be received by those who need it.

There are men of God who have learned the law of faith, which allows them to cooperate with God's power and bless the lives of others – how to yield to it, how to conduct it, how to store it.

FAITH MUST BE IN TWO PLACES

Romans 10:10 shows the law of faith. It reads, *"For with the HEART man believeth unto righteousness; and with the MOUTH confession is made unto salvation."* This verse shows us that faith must be in two places: in the heart and in the mouth. It's not enough for someone to have faith in their heart – it must also be in their mouth.

We see the law of faith repeated in Mark 11:23 & 24 when Jesus said, *"For verily I say unto you, That whosoever shall SAY unto this mountain, Be thou removed, and be thou cast into the sea; and shall not doubt in his HEART, but shall*

*believe that those things which he SAITH shall come to pass;
he shall have whatsoever he SAITH. Therefore I say unto you,
What things soever ye desire, when ye pray, believe that ye receive them, and ye shall have them."* Again, we see that faith
must be in two places: in the heart and in the mouth.

Jesus didn't say that we will receive what we *believe*, but
He said we will receive what we *say*. Verse 23 tells us that we
can release our faith at the time we *say*, and verse 24 tells us
that we can release our faith at the time we *pray*. We are to
believe that we receive what we need from God at the time
we say or at the time we pray.

Faith *comes* by hearing the Word of God (Romans 10:17),
but faith doesn't *operate* by hearing; faith operates or is
released by speaking – speaking God's Word that is in our
heart. When we *hear* God's Word, we believe, but when we
speak God's Word, we receive.

*The law of faith is believing God's Word in our heart and
speaking it with our mouth, and believing we receive our answer at the time we say or at the time we pray.*

FREE FROM EMOTIONS & PARTIALITY

Another important thing to know is that laws are free
from emotion; emotions don't affect their operation, emotions
don't cause them to work. The law of gravity doesn't operate
because someone becomes emotional and cries. The law of lift
doesn't operate because someone cries, wanting it to work.

Likewise, the law of faith doesn't operate because some-one becomes emotional. Someone may become emotional when faced with difficult circumstances, needing the power of God to operate in their situation, so they cry and pray for God to move in their behalf. But emotions aren't the same thing as faith, and emotions don't cause the power of God to flow – the law of faith is what governs the operation of the power of God and causes power to flow. When we need the power of God to work in our behalf, we must release our faith by believing God's Word and speaking it, believing we receive our answer at the time we say or pray.

Laws are also impartial. The law of gravity and the law of lift will work for anyone, regardless of race, social status, income, education, or family history.

Likewise, the law of faith is impartial. It will work for those who work it, regardless of race, social status, income, education or family history. When we believe God's Word with our heart, speak it from our mouth, believing we receive our answer at the time we say or pray, it will work every time – it's a law!

FLIP THE SWITCH OF GOD'S POWER

Since we are so accustomed to the flow of electricity, we don't get amazed when it *does* flow, but we do get amazed when it *doesn't* flow.

In one of the homes we used to live in, if there were

several appliances being used at one time, it would flip the breaker and cause the power to go off. Regularly, while using the hair dryer, the power would suddenly cut off. When the power would cut off, it always sent me into action. I didn't just sit back and hope it would come back on, but I would immediately go to the garage and flip the breaker switches, then the power would come back on. We were so used to having ongoing access to power in the home, that we weren't amazed when it did flow, but rather, when it didn't flow.

Likewise, we shouldn't be amazed and shocked when God's power *does* flow, but rather, when it *doesn't* flow. If God's power isn't moving toward a situation, we need to find out why. Don't just sit back and hope something happens. Rather, we should go into action with our faith.

Just as I would flip the breaker switch to get the power flowing again in the house after it would shut off, we must turn the switch of faith on to have the flow of God's power. We can't allow it to flip off; we must keep the switch of faith turned on. As we do, God's power will move in response to faith.

Everyday, when I turn on the hair dryer, I don't stand there and say, "Wow, look at that!" I'm not amazed when it works. It's when I flip the switch and nothing happens that I get amazed, for then I know that there are steps I must make to get it working.

Every morning I know I have to turn the hair dryer on if I expect to get it to work and to benefit from it. I don't say,

"I'm tired of turning that hair dryer on. It ought to know by now that I need it to work every morning. Why doesn't it just come on automatically?" No, I know that if I want the hair dryer to work, I must turn it on. It won't come on automatically. I must take steps to turn it on. So it is with God's power. Every time you need God's power to flow, you must take steps to cooperate with it, and give movement to that power.

Someone may think, "God knows I need His power in my situation. Why doesn't it just automatically move?" You must cooperate with God's power on purpose. Just like the hair dryer doesn't come on automatically just because you need it, God's power doesn't flow automatically just because you need it. You must flip the switch of faith for God's power to flow. Although I've been turning on a hair dryer every day for years, I know that I'm still going to have to turn it on again tomorrow if I want it to work for me, no matter how many times I've turned it on in the past.

Likewise with the power of God, if I want it to flow for me each day, I must *continue* to release my faith for it. It's not enough that I exercised faith in the power of God in the past, but I must continually exercise faith. As one minister stated, "Faith must be reborn every day." He was letting us know that we must release or exercise our faith every day.

Someone may ask, "How long do I have to keep believing God over a situation?" As long as you need God's power to flow toward the situation. Don't tire of exercising faith in

God's power.

We're diligent to turn on appliances that we need to use every day, so let's be just as diligent toward God's Word and His power, releasing our faith in it every day.

Chapter Seven

ASSIGN GOD'S POWER

The power of God is present, and God has made us stewards of His power. Whether or not power flows depends on us and not on God. Not only must we mix faith with God's power, but we are to *assign* the power of God. Many are waiting for God to send power to their need, but God is waiting on us to assign His power to our need. God's power is ours for everyday life, to assign it to needs we may face.

One Christian lady tells how God told her and her husband to move to another state to assist her son with the church he had started. Her son came to pick them up and drive them to where he lived. The first day, they had driven for hours, but when they tried to get a motel room for the night, all the motels were full. Finally, in the early morning hours, her son said, "Mother, I'm too tired to keep driving. We're going to have to pull over on the side of the road and sleep."

"No," she exclaimed, "God didn't have us to make this trip so we could sleep on the side of the road. I'll handle this!" So she prayed, "God, we need a room to sleep in. Angels, you go and clear someone out of our room!"

"Okay," she told her son, "the angels are clearing someone out of our room. Drive to the next town." That's faith!

She believed she received at the time she prayed. So they drove about another 30 minutes to the next small town. As they came to the town's only motel, the sign out front read, No Vacancy. She told her son, "Go in and get the key to our room."

"But Mother," her son answered, "the sign says, No Vacancy."

"That doesn't matter. The angels cleared us out a room," she insisted.

Angels are part of God's power that's available to us, assisting us as we carry out God's plan, for Hebrews 1:14 tells us regarding angels, *"Are they not all ministering spirits, sent forth to minister for them who shall be heirs of salvation?"* This woman had sent them forth to assist in her need.

Finally, the son went into the motel office, and in about five minutes returned with a room key. The desk clerk had told him that about 30 minutes before they arrived, a trucker who had rented a room, came to the front desk in the middle of the night and said, "I still have such a long drive to make, and I need to leave," and he turned the room key back in. The desk clerk would ordinarily have waited for the housekeeper to come the next morning to clean the room, but instead, the clerk cleaned the room and it was ready when this family arrived. It was not coincidence that the trucker vacated the room at the time she prayed. But notice that nothing happened until she prayed and released her faith.

The power of God is available to you for your everyday

needs, but it's waiting on you to assign it to your need and release your faith.

When this woman and her family arrived at her son's home, they began looking for a home of their own, and a part-time job for her husband. After about two weeks, they still hadn't found a vacant home or a part-time job. So this woman went upstairs to pray. She said, "God, we need a home of our own to live in, and my husband needs a job. Angels, someone is in our home; go clear them out." (This woman wasn't coveting an individual's home, for she wasn't claiming any particular home, but she was claiming what God had prepared for her.)

After she prayed, God spoke to her and told her the name of a place of business where her husband would find a job. She came downstairs and told her husband what God said, and he went to that place of business. When he pulled up, the owner came out to his car and said, "My employee just quit and I need someone to fill that position. It's a part-time job. Would you like the job?" Of course, he took it. The husband returned to the son's house and told the family about how he got the job.

While he was talking, there was a knock on the door. When the son opened the door, a man stood there who said, "I understand your parents are looking for a home. I have a lady who has rented one of my homes for 10 years, but she told me that just this morning she decided to move in with her son. Would your parents like to rent the home?" Of course, they did. It was no coincidence that the job and the home they needed came to them after this woman prayed and released her faith.

The power of God to supply their needs was there all along, but it was waiting on faith, and when she released her faith, assigning it to their needs, the supply they needed came to them. *All God has provided for you is waiting on your faith.*

Don't confine God's power only to church services. His power is available to you for your everyday needs, and it's waiting on your faith. His power is to us-ward who believe. This woman *assigned* God's power to her needs, and when she did, she got results!

An Atmosphere Conducive to God's Power

The power of God is present everywhere, but it's not moving or in manifestation everywhere. For the power of God to be made available and to come into manifestation, the atmosphere must be right; it manifests in an atmosphere of faith. Someone has to release faith in the power of God so that it can come into manifestation. God's power can't move in an atmosphere charged with doubt and unbelief. God's power must be met with faith.

Since we travel so much, ministering all over the nation, we have an airplane to help us accomplish that. We could never conduct as many meetings as we do every year without our own plane to get us there quickly. (In fact, having our own airplane saves us about 150 travel days per year that would have been spent in commercial airports.)

When we fly our airplane to a city, we can't just land anywhere. We can only land in a location that's suitable to land an airplane. Even though we may see a long paved street that's close to the church where we're preaching, we can't decide to land there just because it's close to the church. That paved street isn't prepared to receive airplanes. We can't see an old abandoned airstrip close to the church and decide to land there. No, it could have weeds growing up, and have a damaged, broken surface. It's not prepared to receive an aircraft. We couldn't see an old dirt road that runs in front of the church and decide to land there. No, the place we can land must be prepared to receive an airplane.

It's the same way with God's power. Although His power is present everywhere, it's not moving and in manifestation everywhere. The atmosphere must be conducive to God's power. Faith sets the atmosphere for God's power to move. Just as an airplane can only land in a place prepared to receive it, the power of God can only manifest in an atmosphere that has been prepared to receive it – an atmosphere of faith.

Chapter Eight

CONTINUE IN FAITH

Cast not away therefore your confidence, which hath great recompence of reward.

For ye have need of patience, that, after ye have done the will of God, ye might receive the promise.

— Hebrews 10:35 & 36 (KJV)

Do not, therefore, fling away your fearless confidence, for it carries a great and glorious compensation of reward.

For you have need of steadfast patience and endurance, so that you may perform and fully accomplish the will of God, and thus receive and carry away [and enjoy to the full] what is promised.

— Hebrews 10:35 & 36 (Amplified)

Verse 35 tells us that there is a "great recompense of reward" for those who don't cast away their confidence, their faith in God's Word. What is the "great recompense of reward" to those who continue in faith? They shall receive their answer.

Verse 36 tells us what we must do to receive our answer – we must *continue* with our faith in God's Word. If we are to continue in faith, we must add patience to our faith, for without patience, faith will quit. We must continue to hold fast to our confession of faith in God's Word in the face of all opposition, believing and confessing daily that God's power is moving and working in our situation, regardless of what we may or may not see and feel. Everyday, we must continue to release our faith in God's power toward our situation or need.

CONTINUE WITH THANKSGIVING

Colossians 4:2 tells us, *"CONTINUE in prayer, and watch in the same with THANKSGIVING."* After you initially pray and release your faith in God's power to work in your situation, you are to "continue" in prayer. You're not going to "continue" by continuing to ask for the same thing over and over, but you're to "continue" with the prayer of thanksgiving. The Word speaks of nine different kinds of prayer, and the prayer of thanksgiving is one kind of prayer; that's the prayer we use as we "continue."

When you initially prayed, bringing your need before God, you were using the prayer of faith or the prayer of supplication. But from the time you initially prayed until the time the answer manifests, you are to employ the prayer of thanksgiving – giving thanks to God for hearing you, and thanking Him that His power is working now in your situation. Thanksgiving and praise is the voice of living faith; it's one of the best ways to release your faith – thanking God for His power that is now working in your situation. Since God's power is activated by faith, power will only be able to flow as long as faith flows. If faith stops flowing, power stops flowing. If faith continues to flow, power continues to flow. That's why we must "continue" with thanksgiving, for that's a primary way faith continues to flow.

Again, Colossians 4:2 tells us, *"CONTINUE in prayer, and WATCH in the same with THANKSGIVING."* We are watching over what we prayed for as we continue to give thanks.

YIELD TO THE POWER WITHIN

Power flows as long as faith flows, but many miss it by thinking that power is only flowing if they can *feel* power flowing. Many don't know what power is. Many think power is something we feel, but that isn't always so. Jesus didn't promise an emotional experience; He promised an endowment of supernatural power when the Holy Spirit comes upon us. *"But ye shall receive power, after that the Holy Ghost is come upon you..."* (Acts 1:8). It's not a matter of *feeling* power; it's a matter of *yielding* to the Holy Spirit. It's a matter of yielding to the power of the Greater One who lives within; releasing faith in the power of the Greater One.

There are times that we can sense the tangibility of the power of God, but even if we don't sense or feel the power of

God, that doesn't mean power isn't flowing. Don't wait for a feeling, but rather express or exercise your faith in God's power and believe that it's working, regardless of whether you feel anything or not.

Those who hold fast to their confession of God's Word, believing that God's power is at work in their situation regardless of what they see, feel and hear, are the ones who will experience God's best. In the face of every adverse circumstance, those who continue to release their faith and give praise to God continually for His power that's working in their behalf will enjoy victory.

Chapter Nine

THE GOOD FIGHT OF FAITH

Faith isn't just for the manifestation of the answer, but faith is for the standing – standing on God's Word when faced with all kinds of opposition that tries to sway you off the Word. When faced with opposition, we are to fight the good fight of faith (I Timothy 6:12).

The good fight of faith that we engage in isn't a fight against the devil; we don't fight him, for Jesus already defeated him. The good fight of faith that we engage in is a fight of words – keeping God's Word in our mouth when circumstances press on us, trying to get us to speak something other than God's Word. The good fight of faith we are engaged in is refusing to be swayed from our stand on God's Word.

Ephesians 6:12 tells us, *"For we WRESTLE not against flesh and blood, but against principalities, against powers, against the rulers of the darkness of this world, against spiritual wickedness in high places."* One definition W.E. Vines Expository Dictionary of New Testament Words gives for the word "wrestle" is *sway*. The devil and his evil spirits seek to sway us off God's Word. We don't fight the devil, but we fight the good fight of faith, refusing to be swayed off God's Word.

We remind ourselves, as we take our stand on God's Word, that the devil is a defeated foe, and he can't defeat us as we refuse to be swayed off God's Word.

We are to continue in faith and continue to give thanks and praise to God for His great power that's in our direction.

STRONG IN THE LORD

How can we keep from being swayed off the Word? The two verses prior to Ephesians 6:12 tell us how we can keep from being swayed by evil spirits.

Ephesians 6:10 tells us, *"Finally, my brethren, be strong in the Lord, and in the power of his might."* We are to be strong in the Lord – not strong in ourselves, but strong in Him. What does it mean to be strong in the Lord? God and His Word are one. To be strong in the Lord is to be strong in the Word, and to be strong in the Word is to be full of the Word. We get full of the Word as we feed on, meditate on, and do the Word. Colossians 3:16 instructs us, *"Let the word of Christ dwell in you richly in all wisdom...."*

Ephesians 6:10 goes on to tell us, *"...be strong in the Lord, and in the power of his might."* The "power of His might" is the Holy Ghost. In other words, be full of the Holy Ghost. One of the best ways to live full of the Holy Ghost is to speak much in other tongues. To "be strong in the Lord and in the power of His might" means to be full of the Word and full of the Holy Ghost. You won't be able to stand strong against the devil as an empty vessel – you must be full. That's how you can keep from being swayed off the Word.

THE ARMOR OF GOD

Not only must we be full of the Word and the Spirit, but Ephesians 6:11 goes on to tell us that we must, *"Put on the whole armor of God, that ye may be able to stand against the wiles* (strategies) *of the devil."* Being full of the Word and of the Spirit, and being fully dressed in the armor of God will keep us from being swayed off the Word.

When you're full of the Word, full of the Spirit, and fully dressed in the armor of God, then you'll be able to do the next two verses in Ephesians 6:13 & 14, *"Wherefore take unto you the whole armour of God, that ye may be able to WITH-STAND in the evil day, and having done all, to STAND. STAND therefore...."* Notice the words in these verses that tell us what we're to do: withstand, stand and stand. We're to take our stand on God's Word and stay there, refusing to be swayed. That's the good fight of faith that we're to be engaged in.

Ephesians 6:13-17 reads, *"Wherefore take unto you the whole armour of God, that ye may be able to withstand in the evil day, and having done all, to stand. Stand therefore, having your loins girt about with truth, and having on the breastplate of righteousness; And your feet shod with the preparation of the gospel of peace; Above all, taking the shield of faith, wherewith ye shall be able to quench all the fiery darts of the wicked. And take the helmet of salvation, and the sword of the Spirit, which is the word of God".*

Ephesians 6:14-17 tells us what the armor is that we're to put on:

1. Girdle of truth – represents a clear understanding of God's Word. It holds the rest of the armor in place. God's Word must abide in you.

2. Breastplate of righteousness – your right standing with God. Jesus made you righteous; He is your righteousness because of what He did for you. You wouldn't be any match for the devil without right standing with God.

3. Feet shod with the preparation of the gospel of peace – to live in victory, you must walk in the light of God's Word. (It's dangerous to come up to light and not walk in it.) Feeding on God's Word brings light and faith. Be a doer of the Word; it will be peace to you, even when surrounded by opposition. Faith means being a doer of the Word, and faith in God's Word is your major defense against Satan's onslaughts against your mind and life.

4. Shield of faith – what you use to quench all the fiery darts the enemy assails against your mind in his endeavor to hold you in the mental arena and out of the Spirit, which is the arena of faith.

Think faith thoughts and speak faith words.

5. Helmet of salvation – the knowledge of your position in God because of your salvation and redemption in Christ. This includes having your mind renewed to know your rights and privileges in Christ. This protects your mind – which is Satan's chief battleground.

6. Sword of the Spirit – using the spoken Word against the enemy. It's the only offensive weapon we have. All the other parts of the armor are defensive.

As we stay full of the Word, stay full of the Spirit, put on the whole armor of God, then take our stand on God's Word, refusing to be swayed off of it, we will stay in peace and be able to overcome all opposition and circumstances.

Chapter Ten

A DIVINE EXPLOSION

And in those days, when the number of the disciples was multiplied, there arose a murmuring of the Grecians against the Hebrews, because their widows were neglected in the daily ministration.

Then the twelve called the multitude of the disciples unto them and said, It is not reason that we should leave the word of God, and serve tables.

Wherefore, brethren, look ye out among you seven men of honest report, full of the Holy Ghost and wisdom, whom we may appoint over this business.

But we will give ourselves continually to prayer, and to the ministry of the word.

And the saying pleased the whole multitude: and they chose STEPHEN, A MAN FULL OF FAITH and of the Holy Ghost, and Philip, and Prochorus, and Nicanor, and Timon, and Parmenas, and Nicolas a proselyte of Antioch:

Whom they set before the apostles: and when they had prayed, they laid their hands on them.

And the word of God increased; and the number of the disciples multiplied in Jerusalem greatly; and a great company of the priests were obedient to the faith.

And STEPHEN, FULL OF FAITH AND POWER, did great wonders and miracles among the people.

— Acts 6:1-8

When we read this passage, we see Stephen stand out among the seven men who were chosen to oversee the business of food distribution among the widows in the church.

Not only did Stephen serve in conducting business for the church, but verse 8 tells us, *"And Stephen, full of faith and power, did great wonders and miracles among the people".* Although the seven men chosen to serve were men of honest report, men who were full of the Holy Ghost and men who were full of wisdom, Stephen was the only one who did great wonders and miracles among the people. Why is he the only one out of the seven to be used this way? Verse 5 tells us that Stephen was a man full of faith and the Holy Ghost. Verse 8 tells us that Stephen was full of faith and power. (To be full of the Holy Ghost is to be full of power.) The Word tells us that all seven of these men were full of the Holy Ghost, so they were all full of God's power. But the Word tells us that Stephen was also full of faith. All seven of these men had power enough to work wonders and miracles, but only one had the faith to do it — Stephen!

It's not enough to have power – you also have to have faith! Power is activated by faith! Faith gives action to power. When you mix faith with God's power, you'll get a divine explosion of wonders and miracles.

Just as a chemist or scientist mixes chemicals together to get a reaction or explosion, when faith is mixed with the power of God, the result will be supernatural – a divine explosion.

Many are asking God or waiting on God to send power to their situation, when the power of God is already present and waiting on them to mix their faith with it. We don't have to coerce God into moving by His power in our behalf, for He's already made His power available to us. We just need to add our faith to it – add our "saying" to it. We are to say that we believe that God's power is working in our behalf.

MIX FAITH WITH THE WORD

Hebrews 4:2 reads, *"For unto us was the gospel preached, as well as unto them: but THE WORD PREACHED DID NOT PROFIT THEM, NOT BEING MIXED WITH FAITH in them that heard it."* When God delivered His people out of Egypt, God told them of the land He had prepared for them, but because they didn't believe what He said, they died in the wilderness without receiving what was theirs all along.

Why did they not receive? They heard what God said, but they didn't mix faith with what He said. God's Word has power, but it must be mixed with faith for it to have an effect. Because they didn't mix their faith with what He said, "the Word preached did not profit them".

Is it possible for the Word not to profit us? Yes, if faith isn't mixed with it. We must mix faith with what God says to us in His Word and with what the Spirit of God may speak to us personally. If we don't, we won't profit from what He says.

These Hebrews delivered from Egypt had one of the greatest pastors and leaders – Moses. They saw astounding miracles God worked to deliver them from Egypt. They saw amazing miracles worked for them on their journey, but still they didn't receive all God had for them. Why? They failed to believe.

This shows us that we can have a wonderful pastor and leader, see mighty miracles, signs and wonders, and still not receive all God has for us if we fail to mix our faith with the Word.

The Word will profit every arena of our lives if we will mix faith with it. How do we mix faith with the Word? Our tongues are the mixer. When we put the Word into our mouths, speaking the Word, that's how we mix the Word into our lives and circumstances.

Speak the Word, no matter what the circumstances, and that Word will profit your life.

Chapter Eleven

MAKING POWER AVAILABLE FOR OTHERS

...The effectual fervent prayer of a righteous man availeth much.

— James 5:16 (KJV)

...The earnest (heartfelt, continued) prayer of a righteous man MAKES TREMENDOUS POWER AVAILABLE [dynamic in its working].

— James 5:16 (Amplified)

The power of God is present everywhere because the Holy Ghost is present everywhere, and wherever He is present, power is present. But just because power is present doesn't mean it's available or in manifestation. It's faith that makes power *available* or *brings it into manifestation* for those who need it; it's faith that gives action to power, causing it to move.

When you pray in line with God's Word and release your faith, that faith gives action to God's power. It's not the *act* of praying that releases power, for many people pray without any results at all because they don't exercise or release faith at the time they pray. It's the faith that you release at the time you pray that gives action to power, making power available to the situation you're praying about. It's not the *act* of praying that's powerful, but it's the *faith* you release when you pray that makes the difference.

Remember how Mark 11:24 reads, *"Therefore I say unto you, What things soever ye desire, WHEN YE PRAY, BE-LIEVE that ye receive them, and ye shall have them."* When you pray, believe. It won't do you any good to pray if you're not going to believe, or release faith when you pray. What are you to believe? You are to believe that you receive the answer at the time you pray. You must believe that things change at the time you pray. You must believe that God's power begins working in that situation at the time you pray.

When you release faith through the avenue of prayer, you make "tremendous power available" according to James 5:16 (Amplified). Notice the wording "tremendous power". That gives us the idea that this power can flow in different measures or degrees. If there can be a tremendous measure of power to flow, then there can be a measure of power to flow that is less than tremendous.

"...The earnest (heartfelt, continued) prayer of a RIGH-TEOUS man makes tremendous power available [dynamic in its working]." If you're born again, then you've been made righteous; you're in right standing with God and you have a right to come boldly into His presence and receive what you

need.

What determines how great the measure of power is that flows? James says, *"The earnest (heartfelt, CONTINUED) prayer...."* When you *continue* to exercise your faith through the avenue of prayer toward a situation, the measure of power that flows increases until it becomes a tremendous measure.

As I said in a previous chapter, you don't continue to ask God over and over to do something in a particular situation, but after you initially ask, you continually thank Him that He *is* moving by His power in that situation; that's one way you continue to release your faith, for praise is the voice of faith.

The prayer of thanksgiving is the prayer you're to offer continually after you pray initially. When you continue to release your faith through the prayer of thanksgiving, refusing to quit, the measure of power that flows increases until it becomes tremendous. When a tremendous measure of power flows, it will be "dynamic in its working".

YOUR FAITH CAN'T RECEIVE FOR OTHERS

Years ago, a pastor told me of a woman in his church whose husband had divorced her 20 years before. While they were married, the wife had gotten saved, but the husband didn't want to have anything to do with God, so he eventually divorced her. For 20 years this woman had been praying for him, believing for him to be born again and for their marriage to be restored, but this had not happened. The pastor encouraged the woman to go on with her life and to quit waiting for her ex-husband to return. (He had even remarried, so it's not right to believe for a second marriage to break up so the first one can be restored.)

But she argued with the pastor, "If my ex-husband doesn't return, then that means that my faith failed, and I refuse to let my faith fail."

The pastor asked me, "What would you tell this woman?"

I answered him, "You tell her that her faith worked!"

"What do you mean that her faith worked?" the pastor asked.

I explained, "She has to understand what her faith will accomplish in the behalf of her ex-husband. James 5:16 says that the earnest, heartfelt, continued prayer of a righteous man makes tremendous power available. That's what her faith did. If she's released faith for him for 20 years, she has been earnest, heartfelt, and continued. Therefore, a tremendous measure of power has been made available to him. Her faith worked. That's all her faith can do for someone else – make God's power available to them. But for 20 years he has resisted that power that her faith made available to him. He wouldn't receive. It's not her faith that failed, it's not God's power that failed, it's not God's Word that failed – it worked! *He's* the one that failed! He wouldn't receive of that power –

he resisted it. Her faith can bring power to him, but her faith can't receive it for him."

As you pray for others, your faith is able to make a tremendous measure of God's power *available* to someone else, but it's up to them whether or not they *receive* that power.

People sometimes misunderstand what their faith can do for someone else. You can always get your faith to work for your own needs, but when it comes to other people, their will and desires play a role. Faith and prayer are not meant to control or change the wills of other people. God won't even do that; He doesn't control people's wills.

Releasing your faith through the avenue of prayer in the behalf of someone else won't change their will, but the power that flows to them as a result of your faith makes it easier for them to make the right decisions. When God's power is moving upon someone, His holy influence will bless them and make it easier for them to make right decisions. Your faith can make God's power available to someone, but *they* still must respond to that power and receive it; your faith can't do that for them.

First Corinthians 7:15 instructs us, *"But if the unbelieving depart, LET HIM DEPART. A brother or a sister is not under bondage in such cases: but God hath called us to peace."*

In this situation, the woman should have just let it go instead of hanging onto that desire, and not wasted those years waiting for a spouse who didn't want to come back, but rather, let God give her a husband who would want her. (God knows if someone will turn and repent, so the Spirit may lead someone to stand for their marriage to be restored. But in this situation, the man had already remarried and the Spirit didn't lead her to stand for the marriage to be restored. She was still standing for it only because she misunderstood what her faith could do for someone else.)

THE ROLE OF YOUR FAITH

Some people will begin to question and doubt God's Word and the message of faith after they pray for someone who doesn't receive their answer.

When I pray for someone, I understand the role that my faith plays in their behalf. I know that my faith can make God's power available to them, but I can't receive it for them.

When praying for someone who may be sick and near death, I know that with my faith I can make power available to them; I don't doubt that. But whether or not they respond to that power and are healed is up to them, not me. So, I don't touch whether or not they are healed in my thought life. If they don't receive their healing, I don't take it personally, and I don't start accusing my faith or God's Word of not working. No, I understand the role of my faith for someone else, and that's to make power available to them. It's *their* role to receive that power. So, whether or not they receive is between them and God.

If I prayed for them, releasing my faith in their behalf, then I can rejoice and be confident in God and His Word, for that's all my faith is meant to accomplish in their behalf. If they, for some reason, failed to receive their answer or healing, I refuse to allow that to disturb my faith. Whether or not they receive their answer isn't the role of my faith, that's their role.

Don't touch other people's failure to receive or to be healed in your thought life, for that will weaken your faith. Understand that your faith can accomplish much in the behalf of others, for the tremendous measure of power that can flow to others when you pray is dynamic in its working; it will bring great blessing to people. But also understand that what they believe and desire also plays a role in what they receive from God.

The more proficient and skillful we become with faith and with conducting God's power, the more we'll be able to cooperate with God and bring blessing to others, as well as to our own lives. Let's be bold and faithful to add our faith to this exceeding, great power that's in our direction, and God's power will be a flow of our everyday lives.

SINNER'S PRAYER TO RECEIVE JESUS AS SAVIOR

Dear Heavenly Father:

I come to You in the Name of Jesus. Your Word says, *"...him that cometh to me I will in no wise cast out"* (John 6:37). So I know You won't cast me out; but You will take me in, and I thank You for it.

You said in Your Word, *"...If thou shalt confess with thy mouth the Lord Jesus, and shall believe in thine heart that God has raised him from the dead, thou shalt be saved...For whosoever shall call upon the name of the Lord shall be saved"* (Romans 10:9,13).

I believe in my heart that Jesus Christ is the Son of God. I believe Jesus died for my sins and was raised from the dead so I could be in right-standing with God. I am calling upon His Name, the Name of Jesus, so I know, Father, that You save me now.

Your Word says, *"...with the heart man believeth unto righteousness; and with the mouth confession is made unto salvation"* (Romans 10:10). I do believe with my heart, and I confess Jesus now as my Lord. Therefore, I am saved! Thank You, Father.

HOW TO BE FILLED
WITH THE HOLY SPIRIT

Acts 2:38 reads, *"...Repent, and be baptized every one of you in the name of Jesus Christ for the remission of sins, and ye shall receive the GIFT of the Holy Ghost."* The Holy Ghost is a gift that belongs to each one of God's people. Jesus is the gift God gave the whole world, but the Holy Spirit is a gift that belongs only to God's people.

Jesus told His disciples, *"But ye shall receive POWER, after that the Holy Ghost is come upon you: and ye shall be witnesses unto me...* (Acts 1:8). When you're baptized with the Holy Spirit, you receive supernatural power that enables you to live victoriously.

INDWELLING VS. INFILLING

When you're born again, you receive the indwelling of the Person of the Holy Spirit. Romans 8:16 tells us, *"The Spirit itself beareth witness with our spirit, that we are the children of God."* When you're born again, you know it because the Spirit bears witness with your own spirit that you are a child of God; He confirms it to you. He's able to bear witness with your spirit because He's in you; you are *indwelt* by the Spirit of God.

But the Word of God speaks of another experience subsequent to the new birth that belongs to every believer, and that is to be baptized with the Holy Spirit, or to receive the *infilling* of the Holy Spirit.

God wants you to be full and overflowing with the Spirit. Being filled with the Spirit is likened to being full of water. Just because you had one drink of water doesn't mean you're full of water. At the new birth you received the indwelling of the Spirit – a drink of water. But now God wants you to be filled to overflowing – be filled with His Spirit, baptized with the Holy Ghost.

Acts 2:1-4 reads, *"And when the day of Pentecost was fully come, they were all with one accord in one place. And suddenly there came a sound from heaven as of a rushing mighty wind, and it filled all the house where they were sitting. And there appeared unto them cloven tongues like as of fire, and it sat upon each of them. And they were all FILLED with the Holy Ghost, and BEGAN TO SPEAK WITH OTHER TONGUES, as the Spirit gave them utterance."*

When these disciples were filled with the Holy Ghost, they began to speak with other tongues as the Spirit gave them utterance; they spoke in a language unknown to them. Today, when a believer is filled with the Holy Ghost, they too will speak with other tongues. These are not words that come from the mind of man, but they are words given by the Holy Spirit; these words float up from their spirit within, and the person then speaks those out.

What is the benefit of being filled with the Holy Ghost with the evidence of speaking in other tongues? First Corinthians 14:2 reads, *"For he that speaketh in an unknown tongue speaketh not unto men, but unto God...."* When you're speaking in other tongues, you're speaking to God – it is a divine means of communicating with your Heavenly Father. This is one of many great benefits.

Matthew 7:7-11 reads, *"Ask, and it shall be given you… FOR EVERY ONE THAT ASKETH RECEIVETH…what man is there of you, whom if his son ask bread, will he give him a stone? Or if he ask a fish, will he give him a serpent? If ye then, being evil, know how to give good gifts unto your children, HOW MUCH MORE SHALL YOUR FATHER WHICH IS IN HEAVEN GIVE GOOD THINGS TO THEM THAT ASK HIM?"*

In this passage, Jesus is saying that when you ask God for something, you shall receive! Believe that He will give you that which you ask for. When you ask God for something good, He won't give you something that will harm you; He will give you the good thing you ask for. The baptism of the Holy Spirit is a good gift, and when you ask God to fill you with the Holy Spirit, you won't receive a wrong spirit; you will receive this good gift, the gift of the Holy Spirit.

Once you receive the gift of the Holy Ghost, you can yield to this gift any time, speaking in other tongues as often as you choose; you don't have to wait for God to move on you. The more you speak in other tongues, the more you will benefit from this gift. By continuing to speak in other tongues on a daily basis, you will be able to maintain a Spirit-filled life; you will live full of the Spirit.

The more you take time to speak in other tongues, the deeper you'll move into the things of God.

(For more teaching on being filled with the Holy Spirit, I recommend *Why Tongues?* by Kenneth E. Hagin.)

PRAYER TO RECEIVE
THE HOLY SPIRIT

"Father, I see that the gift of the Holy Spirit belongs to Your children. So, I come to You now to receive this gift. I received my salvation by faith, so now I receive the gift of the Holy Spirit by faith. I believe I receive the Holy Spirit now! Since I'm filled with the Holy Spirit now, I expect to speak in other tongues as the Spirit gives me utterance, just like those in Acts 2 on the Day of Pentecost. Thank You for filling me with the Holy Ghost."

Now, words that the Spirit of God gives you will float up from your spirit. You are the one who must open your mouth and speak those words out. The words will not come to your mind, but they float up from your spirit. Speak those out freely.